MW00878448

MBA 360

by Dr. Shaan Kumar

Published by

K- Publications

Los Angeles, California

MBA 360

by Dr. Shaan Kumar

ISBN: 978-1461116011

Published by: K- Publications, Los Angeles, California

Printed by:

First Printing, 2011

Who MUST read this book?

This book is a handy guide for employees looking to expand their skills and potential. It helps them jump-start their careers and take the fast track to management. It is also a great tool for employers to teach their employees how to align their efforts with those of the company, and accomplish their goals and tasks efficiently and in an organized manner.

For any manager looking to get ahead, this book is a must. It lays out a specific roadmap to achieve his or her career goals. The same goes for entrepreneurs, students, and graduate school aspirants. The principles in this book form the basis for parlaying their energy in a focused manner to attain their business aspirations.

Highlights

MBA 360 begins by describing the basics of management. It gives you simple, highly effective tools that can be applied to your management or business goals in minutes, creating an effective method to track, monitor and control all the activities of your business. It follows this business theory with specific skills you need to develop and how to develop them. It then adds the theory and practice of applying those skills to the problem of business. It teaches today's people skills, technologies, and promotion methods, without rehashing old-school business practices. In brief, it gives the 21st century manager or entrepreneurial leader everything it takes to succeed in his or her career or business.

Whether you plan to become the next Bill Gates or simply want a better job, if you apply the simple, straightforward techniques explained in this book, you cannot help but succeed.

Table of Contents

Chapter 1

MBA 360

Mastering Business Applications in the 21st Century

Bill arrives at work right on time. He grabs a cup of coffee and sits down in front of his computer. He replies to a few emails, clicks on a Facebook video, swaps news with his friends, tweets a message and takes care of a few other tasks. Before he even notices the time passing, it's time for the mid-morning coffee break, where Bill chats with some friends about what happened on TV last night and remembers he wants to download a video he'd forgotten to yesterday.

By the time noon rolls around, Bill looks up and wonders what happened to the morning. He's accomplished exactly nothing. "There just isn't enough time to get everything done," he comments, as he heads out to lunch.

That same morning William arrives just behind Bill. Instead of going to his email inbox, William makes a circuit of the office, greeting everyone, then grabs a cup of coffee, pulls out his Daily Action Plan and focuses on the first item.

By the time mid-morning coffee break time rolls around, William has completed the top five items on his action plan.

Which of these sounds like your day? Way too many people will say it's like Bill's, not William's. Yet the Williams of the world are the ones succeeding. They're the ones who get the promotions, who succeed in their own businesses and accomplish their goals.

Start every day with an action plan. It need not be complex; a list of action items is enough. Only include items that will most affect your business or job. Skip the "would be nice if..." items. Those are fine for fillers in the afternoon after your important tasks are complete.

An action plan is best developed not when you sit down in the morning to start your day, but at the end of the previous day. The best time might be just before you go home in the evening, or possibly before you go to bed, but it is most effective when the day's events are over and still fresh in your mind rather than when the next day is already started.

To succeed in the business world, there are ten applications or business habits that you need to master. Those who can accomplish these succeed; those who ignore them have a far more difficult time. These include the following:

Planning - There are two types of planning: the daily action plan and a longer term career plan, or Vision – Planning – Action plan (VPA) that encompasses a much wider scope. You should always have a VPA that you refer to frequently, and you should start every workday with your daily action plan – just a few items in a written list. The most dog-eared document on a Japanese business executive's desk is his company's 5-year plan.

How many American executives can even find theirs? This is how Japan went from being nearly completely destroyed in WWII to being the second largest economy in the world by the 1980s.

Team, Tasks, Targets, Timelines (4T) - Organization and task management is critical to the success of a modern manager. No longer can a business manager dole out instructions and plans off the top of his or her head. The world has gotten too complex. Fortunately we live in a time where simple, automated systems can ensure these tasks are organized and that all team members are working toward the common goal.

POWER Skills - the five POWER skills are: 1) Presentation- the ability to present yourself effectively in-person and in writing. 2) Opportunity- recognize when opportunities make sense. Creating opportunities is an essential power skill. 3)Wealth- manage all of your resources, not just money, including the talent and capabilities of yourself and your teammates. 4) Entrepreneurial skills- these go beyond mere business management capabilities. Being an entrepreneur encompasses much more. 5) ROI skills: understand that you need a return on investment with the money you invest as well as other capital like time and attention. Recognize that loss occurs when you expend capital on activities that yield a lower rate of return.

Internet - The Internet has become the single biggest influence in business in the 21st Century. Prior to the turn of the century the Internet was a handy way for academics to trade scientific information. The explosion that began in the 1990s continues to this day, converting it from a clumsy file sharing system to the center of the universe of business. On the Internet we now perform all business functions from sales and marketing, to communication, to resource management, to accounting, to personnel.

Mastery of the Internet and its manipulation is perhaps the single most valuable skill you can possess in the business world today.

Digital Media Marketing – The seven largest digital media marketing channels of the 21st century are: 1) Internet, 2) Mobile, 3) E-mail, 4) Social Media, 5) Video, 6) TV, and 7) Radio. Having skills in these types of media are critical to your success in 21st-century business.

Management – There have been numerous theories and practices of modern management forwarded over the past few decades. Many of these succeed and some are dismal failures, although nearly all have their positives. Different management techniques work better with some people than others. Having an effective arsenal of management skills to use in a variety of situations is critical to 21st century businesspeople.

Technology – No matter what business you are in, here in the 21st century, you need to use technology. Modern technology has taken so many of the mundane and difficult tasks that businesspeople have struggled with and made them executable with the click of a button. No longer are teams of clerks needed to do business. Entire departments, once comprised of dozens of full-time people, can now be handled by one person in a few minutes per day. Embrace technology and you succeed; shun it and you don't.

Networking – Even though the Internet had made many business dealings less interpersonal, modern business leaders find it necessary to have larger networks of business associates, mentors, contacts, and friends as these people prove more and more critical to their success. Networking is a skill and a habit – one very worth cultivating.

Entrepreneurial Leadership – Leadership and management are very different qualities and require the development of very different skills.

If you're content to be a middle manager in a mundane company you could probably do so without many entrepreneurial leadership skills. On the other hand if you want to excel in the corporate world, your own business, politics, or even in the social realm having leadership skills will take you far. Entrepreneurship means taking ownership of your job. This is the only way you can strike out on your own. It is also the primary trait top management recognizes when selecting managers for promotion. Take ownership of what you manage and you will succeed.

Sir Isaac Newton, the founder of modern physics said, "If I have seen farther than others, it is because I have stood on the shoulders of giants." There simply isn't enough time in your or anyone's life to make all the mistakes you'll need to make to learn everything you'll need to know to succeed by trial and error. Even if you could why should you? Advanced learning is standing on the shoulders of giants. It allows you to learn from other people's mistakes as well as successes instead of having to learn each of them the hard way. If you take advantage of that you will be miles ahead of others that don't use that advantage. Earn your MBA or any Masters Degree.

This book will discuss these applications indepth so that you can succeed in business or as a career manager. Like playing sports– if you focus on the basics and execute them well the results are far easier to realize than if you just head off into the wilderness with neither a map nor survival skills.

If you incorporate these elements into your

business persona you will become an indispens-able member of your organization.

At some point in your lifetime you should aim to earn your master's degree. With it, you will be able to put these principles to work and acceler-ate your earning potential and career success.

To conclude, remember these points: you will never get time back. Once you waste it, it's gone forever. Learn to manage time wisely so that it will be much easier for you to spend it on what-ever you wish later in life. There will be a lifetime of returns on investments if you spend your younger years wisely developing yourself and your career.

Chapter 2

MBA

The Most Popular Degree in the World

Harvard University first conferred the Master of Science in Business Administration degree in 1908. It was an outgrowth of a previous degree called the Master of Science in Commerce offered by the Tuck School of Business of Dartmouth University in 1900. After this highly respected university offered the degree, the title "Master of Business Administration" stuck and carries forward to this day.

It took until 1957 until an MBA program was offered in Europe. INSEAD (Institut européen d'administration des affaires), a university originally based in Fontainebleau, near Paris, France, was the first to offer MBAs in Europe. Since then, the MBA degree has experienced explosive growth in the US and all over the world. Today, the Master of Business Administration degree is the most popular master's degree by a substantial margin.

MBAs differ from other types of master's degrees because they can be earned by anyone with any undergraduate degree, from the liberal arts through the technical degrees as well as those studying business as undergraduates. No other master's degree appeals to such a wide range of undergraduate studies. Those seeking a master's degree in a science, for instance, almost invariably have a bachelor's degree in that science.

This is true of nearly all master's degree candidates, with the exception of MBA students. Applicants for MBA degrees are more likely to have bachelor's degrees in engineering, science, liberal arts, law, or something similar.

A Master of Business Administration degree confers the essential skills of business to the student. Every business must deal with the same elements, no matter how small or large it is. Whether you're General Electric or a one-person computer programming company, business skills must be employed for your business to thrive and grow. Failing to address business issues that arise can make the difference between prosperity and bankruptcy. An MBA graduate is better equipped to deal with the rigors of business when applying technical undergraduate studies to the real world, regardless of whether that person is an employee or self-employed.

A dentist, chef, architect, or other technical specialist may be extremely competent in a chosen field, but that doesn't mean these professionals can start their own businesses and deliver those services successfully. The MBA gives those seeking to provide independent professional services a strong base of business knowledge to launch, operate and manage their own businesses. It also provides the tools to help these businesses grow and prosper.

For those seeking fast tracks into corporate management, an MBA provides a very empowering addition to their resumes. It conveys prestige and also provides useful knowledge. Many executives consider an MBA to be a prerequisite to hiring an employee as an upper-level manager in their firms. While there are those who naturally understand some business concepts, engaging in a formal study of these principles ensures that the basics are well covered and that the most effective methods and techniques are passed on to the student, leading to a greater potential for success.

Since the entire subject is so vast and no degree can possibly cover all of the possible aspects of such a wide topic, the MBA should not be considered a mastery of the topic of business. It lays the groundwork for successfully managing a business rather than supplying everything that will ensure success at the endeavor. A person with a Master's in Business Administration will have the benefit of their professors and teaching examples to draw upon as well as the advantage of having worked out the example business problems. What the MBA graduate will not have, however, is an insurance policy guaranteeing success in business. It is a license to learn.

There are now a wide variety of different types of MBAs offered. There is the generalized MBA, but there are also MBAs offered in specific business fields, for instance, health care, hospitality, real estate, manufacturing, and so on. Each applies the generalized topics to specific business disciplines. If you are quite certain about the direction you wish to take, select one of these types.

There is also an international MBA that focuses on global business practices. Many aspects of business are very different abroad than they are in the United States. Accounting, banking, and the influence of politics on business (permitting, tariffs, etc.) can vary considerably from country to country. Different philosophies, laws, traditional methods, and outlooks on business can be both different and similar from one country to another. International MBAs offer study materials explaining and expanding on these differences.

Executive MBAs are another relatively new but hugely popular and effective course of study. Executive MBAs are for people midway through their career and are particularly useful since those individuals have learned a lot about real business. These degrees arm them with new tools and effective techniques so they can more fully exploit their existing real world knowledge in business.

Learning in a time-tested on-campus educational setting is the traditional method of obtaining any degree, including the Masters in Business Administration. An on-campus MBA offers an interactive learning experience with lots of social interaction; however, it requires a strict adherence to a learning schedule and a close proximity to the institution you plan to attend. This is not always a good option, especially for mid-career professionals who still have to work while obtaining their degree and who may also have to juggle family obligations. On-campus MBAs also tend to cost the most.

The online MBA is the most rapidly growing method of earning a master's in business. These are an outgrowth of the distance learning or correspondence courses of yesteryear. Online learning has proven to be as effective and in some cases more effective than traditional learning methods. Many traditional universities offer your choice of on-campus or online versions of every course they offer. The Massachusetts Institute of Technology, one of the premiere technical universities in the world, was one of the first to offer every class in their schedule in an online learning format as well as on-campus.

Some of the advantages of obtaining an online MBA include the ability to set your own schedule and work at your own pace. For the less disciplined this may not be ideal, but for those committed and who have other ongoing life obligations, this is a very viable option. In addition, an online MBA is less costly than a traditional one. There is little social interaction and two-way discussion ability, and you may have to wait some time for clarification on something you may not understand.

Whichever method you choose, a Master's is a worthwhile endeavor.

It shows your employer that you are serious about your career, it gives you tools to master your business environment, and it gives you a confidence and sense of accomplishment you cannot otherwise achieve.

Michael Saenz had a long and distinguished career as a plastics engineer. He received an associate's degree, a bachelor's degree, and a masters degree in the aerospace field as he was starting out. Twenty-five years later, his industry suffered a severe downturn that sent the majority of the highly skilled career professionals packing, so he changed direction. He recognized that health care would be increasing in demand as the huge number of baby boomers started aging. He became an administrator of a nursing home and after a few years, realized he needed to know more.

With one master's degree already under his belt and in mid-career, Michael enrolled in California Intercontinental University's Master's in Business Administration program, with a specialty in health care management. The online program allowed him to study at his own pace while he continued working. He graduated with his master's in 2010 and has nothing but praise for Cal University's methods and practical applications.

Marc Larouche successfully completed his Master of Business Administration with a specialization in Information Systems and Knowledge Management in 2009. He did it while working full-time for the Department of Veterans Affairs. Distance education was the only way for Marc to achieve his goal of earning a master's degree. Upon receiving his MBA, he earned a Quality Step Increase and a significant pay raise. Marc has earned certifications in IT Security and has developed courses in both Computer Forensics and Linux Administration. He is currently working on a teaching certification.

Marc has worked with document management systems since Microsoft's first product, and he implemented the very first system into the Department of Veterans Affairs.

Marc has an impressive academic record. Upon receiving his MBA, he earned a quality step increase and a significant pay raise. Marc has earned certifications in IT security and has developed courses in both computer forensics and Linux administration. He is currently working on a teaching certification.

The Distance Education and Training Council recognized Marc as a Famous Alumnus in 2010. They published his story along with several dozen others in their Outstanding Graduates and Famous Alumni publication of 2011.

MBAs are available to anyone at every career level or in any life situation.

Chapter 3

VPA 360

Vision, Plan, Action

For you to go anywhere in your career or business, you need to follow a basic sequence of action that acts as an overriding impetus, accelerating you along your career path. This is Vision, Plan, Action (VPA), which combines three elements into a unified approach that will help you achieve your goals.

Your first step on the path is having vision. Helen Keller once said that the most pathetic thing she could think of was someone who has sight but no vision. Vision means envisioning yourself achieving your goals. It means dreaming big. Having a Big Hairy Audacious Goal (BHAG) is a major part of achieving those goals. This vision is only a dream, but firmly affixing it in your mind is how your built-in success mechanism operates to achieve it.

The same is true of business. Having your ideal scene firmly affixed in your mind is critical to achieving it. This is an activity that needs to be taken seriously—sorting out exactly where you want to go before heading there. To the businessperson, entrepreneur or manager, that vision needs to be formalized. It needs to be written down.

This is one of the primary functions of a business plan, a document every business needs regardless of whether it is seeking outside funding.

All members of the team—from the top managers to the minimum-wage line workers—need to be aware of, and signed on to, the vision. Think of this as the many rowers of a boat. Yes, the helmsman is steering, but if every rower is pulling an oar in a different direction, the boat might not actually arrive it its destination—regardless of the steering. However, if everyone is pulling in the same direction, the helmsman's job becomes easy.

The manager is the helmsman of the project. The job becomes so much easier if all of the oarsmen (the workers) are pulling in the same direction. In the past, companies often kept their workers in the dark, thinking that the workers didn't need to know the overall plans of the organization. The job of management became so difficult, it is no wonder companies of the past were so slow and difficult to manage. The twenty-first century has changed that. Agile companies require a common, shared vision.

From the vision come plans. Plans are formal, documented, written road maps of how to arrive at goals. Plans give everyone a list of items that need to be completed to accomplish projects. Plans also give handy reference points upon which to evaluate progress toward the goal. With a road map, you not only know how you are going to get where you want to be, but you also have ways to measure where you are at any given instant. As we'll discuss in a future chapter, the ability to quickly and accurately measure your progress is critical.

Many aspects of plans will never be executed. This is expected. Never consider unused plans a waste of time, though. Having a Plan B and Plan C are essential. The very act of planning itself increases the chances that, even if an unplanned snag arises, you will have the ability to respond to ever-changing conditions. Dwight D. Eisenhower, the supreme commander of the Allied Forces in WWII, said that plans are nothing, but planning is everything. Of course you'll run into unexpected things, and that may throw off your previous plans, but if you are continually planning, looking at potential options, and adjusting your master plan to accommodate new things that arise, you are creating agility.

Plans need to turn into action. Believe it or not, the vast majority of business plans never come about because people never start. As a venture capitalist, I see all kinds of business plans. Nearly all have merit, but so many of the architects of these plans simply lack the will to start. Many could have been well along even before I ever saw the business plans, but nothing tangible was ever done. I would much rather fund a less lucrative business plan from someone who has started and is making do without the capital they need to realize the entirety of the plan than fund someone who has grand ideas and a business plan that will confer great wealth on the investors, but who won't start until conditions are just perfect. I know the former will execute his plan with much more certainly than the latter.

This cycle of Vision >Plan >Action is how all of my companies are structured. The USGEA, K-Publications, and the rest of my ventures all incorporate VPA as an integral part of their management systems.

The concept of VPA has been accepted by the Academic Council of CalUniversity and has been implemented across the university program delivery model. Before enrollment, the students integrate a VPA plan into their own educational careers. At the beginning of each class, VPAs are performed for that class, and the students apply the VPA concept right through until graduation. VPA is used for every degree level, including bachelors, masters, and doctoral students. Using it, the university has one of the highest success and graduation rates in the industry. Listening to the program's rave reviews by both the graduates and their employers, CalUniversity seems to be on the right track. VPA is an integral part of students' success.

Chapter 4

POWER Skills 360

**Presentation, Opportunity, Wealth,
Entrepreneurial, ROI**

There are few people in the Western world interested in self-improvement or business who haven't heard of Tony Robbins. Robbins has served as a personal guru to presidents, Fortune 500 CEOs, entertainers, and millions of other people. He has the honor of having sold more audio recordings than Michael Jackson.

Robbins grew up in a poor suburb of Los Angeles and was kicked out of his house by his parents when only 17 years old. Destitute, Robbins decided that sales was an area in which he could make some money; so, rather than take a job with a guaranteed salary (such as flipping burgers or doing manual labor), he started selling tickets to entertainment events. Robbins quickly discovered he had an incredible natural talent for persuasion. In the early 1980s, he came across neurolinguistic programming, a way of programming yourself to achieve your goals, and parlayed that concept into the incredible success he is today.

Tony Robbins became a gifted speaker. He now loves being in front of people, presenting his ideas. It wasn't always that way, however.

He had to work hard and hone his natural talent into real skills. Having presentation skills is a must for anyone in the field of business, whether sales person, executive, manager or entrepreneur.

Public speaking is a scary prospect for many people. In fact, it is the second most feared activity, right behind going to the dentist. Imagine that: people fear speaking in front of an audience even more than bungee jumping or skydiving. Here's the good news, though: public speaking is not an innate talent, but a learned skill. People learn this skill by doing. The more you speak in public, the less self-conscious you are about it.

There are many ways to learn how to present yourself verbally. Take a debate class, or join Toastmasters International (an organization with the sole purpose of teaching people how to speak in front of others). Or teach a class in a field you are familiar with. It doesn't matter what topic, only that you stand in front of others and get your point across to them. You'll quickly find out that when you focus on your subject matter, you forget about your anxieties.

You need to learn how to express yourself in other ways besides speaking – developing writing skills, for instance. Like speaking skills, writing skills are learned, not innate. Most writers had to learn how to write; they weren't born with the ability. Of course, many great writers have natural-born talent. But as a business manager, executive or entrepreneur, you don't need the kind of artistic skills that great poets, novelists and screenwriters have. You need only to be able to express your thoughts and ideas clearly and with persuasive conviction.

The ability to be organized in your writing is essential in the business world. The key to writing in an organized fashion is to outline first.

This is the equivalent to planning in the VPA sequence discussed in the last chapter. First, you visualize what you are trying to get across, then you plan (create an outline), and finally you perform the action (you actually start writing). Having the outline (plan) allows you to focus on one thought at a time and get across what you are trying to say more easily and naturally. You need not focus on spelling and precise grammar; modern technology will assist you in those areas.

Next, you need opportunity skills. These are skills that allow you to recognize opportunities when they present themselves. Some people believe they have to be lucky to have opportunities pass their way. This is not true – opportunities are created. You need to use your critical thinking skills to look at situations to recognize opportunities where others don't.

Let's look at something most people know how to do: bake cookies. Wally Amos was a talent agent in Los Angeles in 1975 when he recognized an opportunity in selling home-baked cookies. His friends and family told him it was a horrible idea. Sugar prices were high, people were reeling from a recession, and besides, people could buy cookies cheaper in the grocery store or bake them at home. Nonetheless, Wally didn't pay attention to the naysayers and forged ahead. He opened a cookie shop and by his second year was selling over one million dollars' worth of cookies. He then branched out to sell packaged cookies in stores, rapidly expanding his little shop into an internationally recognized brand. In less than four years, Wally "Famous Amos" sold his cookie enterprise and retired wealthy.

There are opportunities everywhere. Learn to recognize them and you will add an important power skill to your arsenal.

Wealth is the next item in the POWER skill shopping cart. Knowing how to cultivate, expend, and use wealth is a must for business success. Wealth is not only money; it is resources. Money is only one aspect of wealth. Wealth also encompasses time, energy, talent, experience, opportunity costs, and other business resources. How do you allot your time? We're only given so much of it. Do you put it to good use? Could you be using your time more efficiently? How about your assets—the machines that produce your goods? Would it be better to put them to use doing something else and establish an outside supplier to take over their jobs?

A competent businessperson is a master of resource management. He or she is constantly asking questions about how to more efficiently use the resources at his or her disposal: the people, the time, the talent, and—yes—the money. It is currently tied up in inventory, tooling, work in progress, accounts receivable, and other cash-guzzling endeavors. Can it be used more productively?

Entrepreneurial skill is another piece of the business or career success puzzle. Having entrepreneurial skills means much more than simply being a good business manager. It means combining management know-how with technical competence in every area of a business and wrapping it all in a healthy dose of passion and willingness to do whatever it takes to get the job done. Entrepreneurs rise to the top in every organization. Their willingness to look at the big picture and utilize management skills, as well as their drive to succeed, put them way ahead of the usual nine-to-five employees who spend their days filling office chairs.

Of course, many people with entrepreneurial skills get fed up with the corporate grind and strike out on their own. However, many companies also recognize the value of people with entrepreneurial skills, so they provide these people with environments that allow their talents to flourish. People find out quickly whether they fit into the company culture or are destined to be in business for themselves.

Like other skills, entrepreneurial skills are learned. People can develop their entrepreneurial tendencies. They should start out with a healthy dose of skepticism and a willingness to make waves, but once they overcome the basic fear of getting dumped, these people will find that most companies welcome their entrepreneurial spirit and support their efforts to make improvements. It begins with the premise of nothing ventured, nothing gained.

Cultivate your entrepreneurial spirit. Care about the success of your company and your team. Look at new ways to solve problems, and do so with an eye towards benefiting your company, not yourself. An entrepreneur is willing to research, learn, synthesize and apply knowledge to his or her business. Spend the effort, regardless of whether the business is owned by you or someone else. Do so and you'll succeed—even in the largest, most staunchly structured corporations. The big problem is that once you acquire these skills and start practicing them, you realize how much better you could do on your own. That is how new businesses are started—by people who see how well even relatively inept businesses do and realizing that they can do those things that much better.

Finally, ROI skills complete the POWER skill set. ROI stands for return on investment. It isn't big news that people expect a return when they invest in something. Who would buy a stock or bond without the expectation of getting more back in return, and who wouldn't put money in an investment that pays 8% over one that pays 6%?

However, having ROI skills means much more. It is natural to use ROI thinking when discussing money matters, but what about other assets? How do you get the most ROI for your or your employee's time? How do you get the most from your inventory or machines?

ROI skills have a lot in common with wealth management skills, but add an additional twist, looking at the return you receive when using those assets in a certain way. For instance, it may be wise to put all of your personnel assets into completing a not-so-profitable job if impressing the customer will result in more profitable business in the future. In other words, investing your time in a long-term profitable venture now may have a better ROI than putting it into a short-term project that has a better immediate profitability but no long-term return.

Everything in your sphere of influence needs

to be examined for ROI. Think about how to get the most out of something by putting the least amount in. That is what stellar management performers do. They carefully weigh how to best use their assets for the best return on investment.

Tony Robbins is reaping the huge return on investment of his time and efforts put in when he was young. He now has an enormous posh villa on the island of Fiji where he and his family can relax for three or four months a year. He still delivers his self-help program to many celebrities and regular folks, but he is certainly enjoying the return on his investment.

Chapter 5

Task 360

Tasks, Team, Target, Time-line

Managing projects to completion is the whole point of any type of business management. Project management may be broken down into the 4 Ts: Tasks, Team, Target, and Time-line.

Each of these needs to be well thought out, defined and put into play to arrive at the successful completion of anything. A skilled manager must be able to think in these terms and refer continually to these four Ts to keep the project on track and on time.

The first of these Ts is the tasks. Someone, generally the manager in concert with his team members, needs to break the vision into separate tasks. For instance, in the case of a restaurant marketing project, one of the tasks might be to investigate the cost of advertising in local newspapers and magazines and on radio and television. In the case of a new, high-tech manufacturing facility, the task might be to investigate the availability of local vacant warehouse space to house the factory.

Assigning tasks means breaking down the entirety of the vision into small bites, each based in separate disciplines. The architectural task of designing a building shouldn't be combined with the identification of a convenient site to locate the building because they require very separate disciplines to accomplish.

Once you have the tasks, it is time for the second T: team. The correct personnel need to be assigned to each of the tasks. This should be done in accordance with who is most suited to complete each activity. Here's where the wise manager allows input from his or her staff. Allowing people to volunteer for different activities gives them some investment in the program. People are far more likely to be enthusiastic about completing their tasks if those tasks have been requested rather than assigned by their superiors. People's capabilities, strengths and weaknesses need to be considered when assigning tasks; however, willingness to try should be accommodated, even if it means assigning another individual with those skills to oversee or act as a mentor during the activities.

Many things go undone in businesses because people don't realize which tasks are supposed to be done by them. Unless specifically assigned, people assume someone else will do it—so in the end, nothing gets done. Having individuals assigned to do every task makes sure all workers know what is expected of them. This is a powerful incentive, being aware that the team is counting on them to complete a certain task.

Next is the third T: target. Team members need to know what constitutes the completion of their tasks. The target is a major milestone, a clearly defined completion to the task, such as printed fliers ordered or manufacturing building purchased. Bringing clarity to the team benefits everyone concerned.

Attaining targets bolsters morale. I recall that in my university days, I had a flow chart of the classes I needed to take to attain my undergraduate degree. Nothing gave me more pleasure and more incentive than coloring in the completed classes with a highlighter after I received my grades. Watching the colored line progress ever so slowly toward my goal made my progress appear very real, and this boosted me along to the next class. Managing businesses works the same way. When people can see the progress, they can see how what they do contributes to the big picture.

Contrast that to simply assigning someone some random task: "Hey, Mr. Smith, find out how much the newspaper charges for display ads in the sports section."

You're likely to get a response like: "Huh? Me? What?"

Finally, every task needs a timeline, a specific amount of time allotted for the attainment of the target.

The task is assigned a start date and a completion date and is interspersed with milestone tasks. For instance, if the task is to purchase a manufacturing facility, intermediate milestones might be to locate local facility possibilities, decide on first and second choices, make an offer on the first choice, complete negotiations, and start and close escrows. Each of those minor milestones will have a specific deadline so systematic progress can be made toward the ultimate goal.

You must evaluate progress if you expect results. You can't manage what you don't measure, and periodically measuring conformance to the process is one important way to evaluate progress towards a goal. If you see a specific task falling behind, you can do something about it, such as recruit additional help or suggest ways to get back on schedule. Measuring progress allows you to manage only those things that need management. When given motivated and competent team members who know what is expected of them and when, the manager's job is easy—he or she can just supervise what is going on and offer suggestions along the way. When a manager is given a team that isn't knowledgeable about the specifics of the four Ts and whose progress is not being continually measured and monitored, the job becomes difficult, requiring continual assistance to get things done.

Andrew Carnegie, the famous industrialist and founder of U.S. Steel in the early 1900s, was a big believer in measuring what you manage. When brought in to evaluate why a certain steel mill was underperforming, he was given a tour of the factory by the plant manager. When it was time to change shifts, he was standing near the time clock.

Carnegie asked how many heats of steel the

plant had produced that day. The foreman replied with six, so Carnegie took a piece of chalk and wrote a big "6" on the floor by the time clock, then left. When the second shift came in, they asked what the 6 meant and the foreman told them that the big boss had been in and written the number of heats the plant had produced on that floor.

When the day shift came back the next morning, the big "6" had been erased and in its place was a "7." The day shift workers were infuri-ated. Did the night shift guys think they could outdo them? Well, when the night shift came in that evening, the "7" was gone and in its place was a big "9." That'll show those night shift guys who can make steel.

The next morning the day shift came to work and saw a big "11" written in place of the "9." Carnegie had nearly doubled the output of the fac-tory without adding personnel, without issuing any orders, and without reprimanding anyone. He did it practically without uttering a single word. All he did was measure what he wanted to manage. The plant didn't keep up with the frantic pace it had when the two shifts were competing with each other, but it certainly no longer underperformed.

The only way to win is to keep score. Metrics

need to be placed on every aspect of projects, whether it is making steel or giving haircuts. Have you noticed, these days, that everyone wants you to fill out a survey of some kind? Retail businesses give you coupons or the chance to win something simply by filling out a form. This is done for a specific reason.

It's to collect enough information to establish baselines of products and services. It establishes benchmarks of how the business is performing today compared to standards – the minimum of what the business is expected to produce.

The concept of managing by metrics, or things you can measure, while keeping a business's roots in antiquity, was formalized by the work of W. Edwards Demming. Demming was the theoretician to first to use the term total quality management, meaning to assign everything a metric, or something measurable, and to track a business's performance to that standard. The Japanese were eager to adopt this concept in the 1960s and 70s and apply it to their manufacturing. It worked incredibly well.

I met a manager who was asked to take over a Motorola manufacturing facility in Indiana that was having difficulties with quality. The plant had been running a 120 percent rejection rate – in other words, every TV was rejected once, and some twice. A Japanese company purchased the factory, and the new management installed the Demming total quality management techniques and applied metrics to all manufacturing processes. Once the new system had taken hold, the rejection rate had plummeted to only a few TVs per thousand! Using the very same factory with the very same people, and only by changing the management, the company was able to completely reverse a horrific quality trend and realize substantial profits where losses were once the norm.

The chapter on Technology 360 discusses some simple automated tools to track the 4Ts of management. If you learn nothing else from this book, you will learn the importance of managing Tasks, Team, Target and Timeline. There are few more powerful concepts in the entirety of business administration.

Chapter 6

Digital Media 360

Mastering the Seven Channels of Digital Media

In 1924, a man named Claude C. Hopkins published a small book that changed the world. The book is only 41 pages long, but it created such a resounding effect in the business world that its effects are still felt today. You're probably wondering who Claude C. Hopkins is and what he wrote about.

Claude C. Hopkins' groundbreaking book was entitled Scientific Advertising. When it was published in 1924, the business world suddenly "got" what advertising was all about. People generally knew how advertising worked before that. In fact Mark Twain, way back in the 1880s, once

45

said: "The spider looks for a merchant who doesn't advertise so he can spin a web across his door and lead a life of undisturbed peace!" People just didn't know how to use advertising to its fullest extent.

Before Claude C. Hopkins' book came out, advertising was considered merely a way of letting people know you were in business. Whether ads were successful or failed was seen as a matter of sheer luck; or maybe the copywriters and graphic designers simply had a "knack" for putting ads together. Because of Claude C. Hopkins, though, you know what Tony the Tiger thinks of your breakfast cereal, which car is "the ultimate driving machine," and what kind of shoes you should wear if you want to "just do it."

The world today is filled with an overload of advertising noise. We are assaulted constantly by newspaper and magazine ads, billboards, radio spots, TV commercials, and even product placements in TV and movies. We see ads in emails, on Facebook, YouTube, whenever we Google something, when we look up addresses on our smart phones – all the time.

In the past, those with the big bucks got through the noise by pushing the same theme over and over again.

Think of all of the people who were told hundreds, maybe even thousands of times that Budweiser is the king of beers, or not to squeeze the Charmin. These spots cost the advertisers millions upon millions of dollars. What chance does a small upstart business have of competing in that marketplace, hammering brand recognition into people's heads at tens of thousands of dollars per minute? The answer is none.

Fortunately, we now have electronic media. We need only advertise to those people who are seeking our services. The cost per impression (one person viewing one ad) might be higher, but you only show your ad to those who actually may use your product. This is a better approach than (for example) trying to establish brand recognition at convention of rabbis by claiming that pork is the other white meat.

When someone goes to Google and types in "how to give a dog a bath," you can feel relatively confident that he's a pet owner looking for products that enhance his pet's life and its relationship with him. Putting a dog shampoo ad in front of that specific searcher will be far more effective that putting the ad in front of someone Goggling "chicken tikka masala recipes." The new electronic media brings new scientific advertising into play, featuring brand-new concepts that most people over 50 are only vaguely aware of, it at all.

There are seven electronic media channels that you must be familiar with if you intend to be a successful manager or entrepreneur in the 21st century. Let's go through these seven channels and briefly discuss how they're used, and why you need to know about them:

Internet: The World Wide Web, the part of the Internet that you're undoubtedly familiar with, is only a portion of the whole Internet.

The WWW started in the early 1990s but didn't really catch on until the late 1990s. Although it is still less than 15 years old, for most businesses, the internet has changed everything. Having an internet presence (a website) as a method of advertising your business has been considered almost mandatory during the past decade. You may be surprised to learn that (at the time of this writing) only about two-thirds of the small businesses in the U.S. even have a website and fewer than one-third engage in any online e-commerce. The numbers outside the U.S. are even smaller.

Of those who have a website, only a tiny fraction will even bother to figure out how to appear high on the search engine returns. Suppose you were looking for a certified public accountant in Washington D.C. If you type that into a search engine, such as Google, you get over eleven million results. With only 10 results per page, you're looking at over a million pages of information. Statistics show that 70 percent of the people who use a search engine like Google never go past the first page and 97 percent never go past the second page, so what good is your website if you appear on page eight, or page 876, or page 87,654,321? This does you almost no good at all. Only people who are already aware of your business and know its exact name will ever find you. It is important to know and use search engine optimization to get your business on at least page two of the results (and preferably on page one). And no, you can't send a check off to Google and ask them to move you to the head of the class; they rate pages based on merit, meaning you have to earn your way to the top.

It's not particularly difficult. You just need to learn and follow the rules to get there.

In addition to the free advertising you can get by becoming a top result of the search engines, you can also buy pay-per-click, or PPC, advertising spots from the search engines. These are small, one-headline and one-sentence ads that Google presents to people searching the Web to encourage them to click and end up on your Web site. Here's the interesting part: you only pay for those people who actually click on your ad and land on your site, not those who merely look at (or ignore) the ad. PPC has its drawbacks and can be expensive, but it will absolutely drive targeted traffic to your Web site. How you convert the visitors into paying customers is then up to you.

E-Mail: Yes, I know that you are inundated with spam e-mail. Nearly everyone is, and everyone hates them. But using e-mail can be very effective if you use what is known as opt-in methods, where people actually request to be on your mailing list and receive e-mail. These highly targeted e-mail lists work to create a large base of people interested in what you have to say.

By far the most effective way to create large opt-in e-mail lists is to offer people information they are craving. Don't think of the Internet as a giant Walmart where you can sell anything; think of it as an enormous public library where free information is everywhere if you know where to look. Will people sign up to have you hammer them with sales pitches every day? Of course not.

They will, however, sign up to receive weekly gardening tips, recipes, sports information, even money-saving coupons – things that fall within the sphere of what your business offers.

Mobile: You may not have realized it, but very powerful computers have shrunk considerably in the last few years. They are now what we used to call cellular phones. Mobile computing has taken over where the mobile telephone used to be king. Mobile "apps" (really computer programs connected to web sites) are now riding the crest of the advertising wave.

Imagine you're in a strange city. You're hungry and feel like eating pizza. Back in the old days, you would have pulled over to a public phone booth, found a yellow page directory and looked up a pizza parlor. These days, you'd whip out your mobile phone and use an app to find the closest pizza parlor. Given the enormity of what can be accomplished with a computer program, can you imagine just about any business that couldn't offer customers and potential customers an app to help customers do their jobs better, faster, or easier? As a sideline, couldn't the business offer its own product or service as an added bonus?

YouTube: More young people these days sit down in front of YouTube than in front of the television set. That trend seems to be continuing. YouTube videos have received several million hits in a single day. It was back in 2007 that YouTube surpassed Yahoo in the number of searches carried out every day: it is that big a deal.

If you want to get your commercial in front of one million viewers on television, plan on spending six figures for the exposure, at least. That doesn't include the production costs of shooting the commercial. But these days you can put yourself or your product on YouTube for absolutely free.

Not only that, but with modern inexpensive video recorders, you can produce your video for free as well. Whether millions of people tune in and watch it depends on how cleverly you present the information. Again, it's all about targeting your audience. Few people will tune in to watch you pitch a product, but they certainly will to learn something new as described in the email marketing description above.

YouTube also seamlessly integrates into social media sites (e.g., Facebook) and the linking of YouTube videos from your website makes you highly attractive to Google. Since Google owns

YouTube they give credit to websites that use their family of products, so having embedded YouTube pages on your website will earn you bonus points when the search engine is deciding where your site will rank. This is another very effective way to integrate your digital media channels into a larger, more effective overall strategy.

For all of her life, Susan Boyle, a frumpy middle-aged matron from rural England, had wanted to become a professional singer. In 2009, she got her chance to sing on a reality TV show Britain's Got Talent. It was a popular show, but it wasn't exactly lighting the world on fire with a viewership of approximately 1.5 million. Susan did a terrific job. The very next day, close to 10 million people from all over the world watched the YouTube video of her performance. When friends began contacting friends, people began posting, and re-posting Susan's video to their Facebook pages until millions were exposed to her talent. This landed her a major record contract; guest appearances on Oprah and Late Night; makeovers and photo spreads in the major fashion and entertainment magazines; and worldwide renown on a scale never witnessed before.

As of this book's writing, her original

YouTube video has had over 65 million views!

Web TV: An outgrowth of YouTube, integrating television-quality videos into the Internet experience has brought us Web TV. Web TV has a few very special features that make it much more attractive than broadcast or cable TV. Perhaps the most obvious of these is the ability to save the TV shows on your Web site to be viewed by anyone, anywhere. The viewer does not need to record the program or buy a prerecorded disk; he or she can just go to the archives on your Web site and watch it at his or her leisure. Having a Web TV channel is a very effective way to get across information that supports or is supported by your business.

Since it is essentially free, Web TV is the perfect place to advertise yourself. It's where you can establish your brand. Today's successful managers—those who rocket to the top—are good at promoting themselves. There is no shame in this; self-promotion needs to be part of an overall strategy to make yourself stand out among your peers. When you have a familiar persona, you can create a recognizable brand in any industry for any specialty.

Emeril only needs one name, because everyone knows who he is. Is he a great chef? Many say no, but in spite of that he is one of the most famous chefs in the world. People know, like, and follow him. His persona has been established through his TV shows. He didn't do those shows to promote his restaurants; he did them to promote himself. It is only natural that career success would follow.

Whether your specialty is a technical product or service or a consumer product or service like Emeril's, or even if you're a middle manager in an unexciting business, getting a following amongst your peers is as much about putting yourself out there and gaining exposure as it is about being a recognized expert.

Web Radio: Like web TV, it has become very easy to set up a web radio station to put forward news, information, and entertainment based on your business's products and services. Like having videos, this form of media is also easily integrated into social media and Web sites, thereby increasing your perceived value by the search engines, resulting in a higher position in the search results. All of these digital channels work in concert to present a strong and effective Web presence. Conversely, a lack of these elements presents a weak and ineffective overall strategy that does more to discourage potential clients than to con-vince them.

Social Media: Google used to be the most visited Web site on the Internet by a long shot. It's not anymore. Facebook has taken over. Social me-dia sites as a whole are the biggest application the Internet has ever experienced. It started with MySpace, mostly a site for children and teens, but these days, Facebook for adults, LinkedIn for pro-fessionals, and Twitter as a micro blog broadcast-ing any message you wish to your friends have pre-sented huge opportunities to market products. These are inexpensive and very effective digital channels for marketing.

Colleges and universities are offering social media marketing classes for those interested in these venues. There are both right and wrong ways to use social media to promote your products or services. When it is used correctly, social media can create an extremely rapid international buzz with potential explosive effects on product expo-sure.

Learning how to promote through social media is not merely important, but in these rap-idly changing times, social networking is a neces-sity for a business manager or an entrepreneur.

In 1960, the world encountered the first person to use the power of television to become President of the United States. John F. Kennedy set the bar for every president following, by using TV as his main campaigning tool: every president, that is, until 2008. In 2008, the candidate relying on TV campaigning lost and the first candidate to rely most heavily on internet marketing methods was Barack Obama. The power of digital media is undeniable.

Obama was all over Facebook in 2008. Friends linked to his home page, posted his videos, commented on what he said, and created the enormous buzz than eventually landed him in the White House. There were rumors that John McCain didn't even use computers (a bit unfair since he had lost use of his right arm because of the torture he underwent as a POW during the Vietnam War). Nonetheless, Obama drew young people to the voting booths like never before, not in small part because of his effective use of social media.

Since Obama's victory, you've seen other potential candidates, like Sarah Palin, turn to Facebook, Twitter and other social networking venues to get messages out to their followers. Even the uprisings in Egypt, Tunisia, and Libya have utilized Facebook as a major communications tool, allowing people to organize, inspire and promote different causes. The fact that social networking is essentially free is part of its astounding power.

One important thing to remember when preparing information for presentation through digital channels – the viewer has control. They can start, stop, fast forward, or navigate away from your information if at any time they feel that they are being pitched to or are bored.

This is very different from a TV commercial that people will patiently sit through because they're waiting to find out who the baby's father is when the daytime soap opera returns from commercial break. That is not the case in the digital world. The information you are presenting must be of interest to viewers; otherwise, they will simply move on. It needs to be short, concise, and realistic—and it must capture the viewer's interest. You can't have long sales pitches; you need to present information the viewer wants, and do so quickly and without commercial content. Emeril doesn't spend lots of time telling you why you should come to his restaurant; he teaches you how to make his famous jambalaya and then kicks it up a notch—BAM!

Businesspeople like to think the Internet is a huge mall where they can simply set up a store and start selling their products, but it is not. It is a big library where enormous amounts of information are all available for free. That's how people use it. Think about how you use the Internet. Do you use Google to find products or to find information? Think as well about the words you use to search. Most attorneys call themselves attorneys, not lawyers, so the word lawyer doesn't appear in their websites. Yet most people searching for an attorney search for lawyer. Having pride in your profession is fine, but don't exclude the majority of your potential customers because of it.

People are looking for information, so give it to them. Publish papers, how-to guides, e-books, and other free information people can use. If you do, they'll appreciate your knowledge and buy from you. If you only deliver your sales pitch, they'll leave without listening.

Master digital media.

You can easily and inexpensively promote your products, your company and yourself. With it, your business can achieve nearly instant success. Millions all across the world can tune into you, and if you have something powerful to say many will admire, follow and listen to you. In the 21st century, this is the most effective way to promote yourself.

Chapter 7

Management 360

Modern business is profoundly different from businesses of the past. Agility, or the ability to make rapid adjustments, has replaced sheer size and consistency as the primary survival mechanism of companies in the past few decades. So many businesses have come and gone, especially in the technology world, that a whirlwind of what seem to be good companies are here one day and gone the next. To master business management is to understand how to be agile.

Jack Welch was named CEO of General Electric in 1981. His influence on the company was nothing short of staggering. GE went from a good, stable, big corporation with a long record of steady growth, to become one of the top performing companies in history. This was accomplished mostly through the efforts of Jack Welch.

Jack Welch felt that if you were going to be in business, you'd better be number one or number two in your industry or else move on to something else. Under his nearly 20-year reign, GE went from amassing 13 billion dollars in revenue to over 200 billion. Though he has his detractors, there is no denying that Jack Welch was one of the most effective business managers of all time.

Welch used a combination of carrot and stick when managing GE. Every year, he ruthlessly chopped the bottom performing 10 percent of his managers, and richly rewarded his top 10 percent with generous bonuses and stock options.

He also earned the nickname Neutron Jack (after the neutron bomb, a weapon that kills people without affecting infrastructure) because of the way he would completely clear out nonperforming divisions, product lines, and other poorly performing parts of the company. While this made him a tyrant to some employees, it made the slow-moving giant called GE. This newfound agility is what prompted the company's enormous growth.

Historically, successful managers utilized the very same skills as successful wartime generals, who acquired their skills from an even older skill – successful hunting strategy, traceable back to the dawn of man. After all, relatively frail humans came to occupy the top of the food chain only by working together and organizing. The animals that cavemen hunted weren't easy prey. They were faster, stronger, more wary, and had better senses than humans, yet humans were able to hunt even the largest and strongest of these animals by applying organizational, leadership, and communications skills, which form what we call management today.

There are four general categories of skills required for management:

Technical Skills: Technical skills encompass the knowledge and experience needed to perform technical tasks. You wouldn't have a successful manager of a laboratory full of chemists if the manager had no knowledge of chemistry. The manager need not be as smart or capable as the brightest Ph.D. chemist on staff, but he or she must know what the workers are doing. He or she needs to be competent enough to understand what is going on and to make adjustments as required. This is true whether the work being performed is highly technical, such as in the medical profession, or whether it is rather mundane, like managing a team of pizza delivery people or lawn care workers.

Political Skills: A competent manager must have political skills to convince his or her team members to participate.

He sometimes needs it in order to convince people who strongly disagree with each other to put aside their differences and find common ground, pushing tasks though to completion. Political skills consolidate power and allow the teams to keep a relevant "big picture" of what their work and the overall business is intended to achieve.

Conceptual Skills: A manager utilizes conceptual skills to analyze complex situations and arrive at solutions based on the input he receives. You don't need crystal ball-reading clairvoyance to see what lies ahead, only an ability to synthesize logical outputs from a wide variety of inputs. Being right a high percentage of the time is desirable, and will certainly get you noticed. However, in most management situations, you need only need to be right more than half of the time, so long as you are able to recover quickly when you realize you're on the wrong path.

Interpersonal skills: Good managers have good people skills. They need not be well-liked, but they should be respected. Employees should know they can count on the manager to back them up, to look out for their individual interests as well as the interests of the company, and to act as a go-between whenever needed. An exceptional manager also has the ability to recognize talent in those reporting to him or her, and to delegate work in a way that ensures the most efficient use of personnel assets.

There are three general levels of Management:

Top Management: sometimes called C-Level, as in Chief Executive Officer, CEO, Chief Operations Officer, COO, and so on. The titles may also be Managing Director, Board Member, Vice President, and so on. These are the people who develop the goals, strategic plans, and general policies of the company.

A person might be a full-time executive on an upper floor of a major corporation's office building. Elsewhere, a person might run the show and clean the restrooms, as is common in small, entrepreneurial operations. Either way, these activities are necessary for the success of the company. It matters not whether time devoted to them amounts to only a few hours per month or is the responsibility for dozens of full-time employees: Conducting these activities in one way or the other is absolutely essential.

Middle management consists of team members who are responsible for getting the work completed. These are generally department managers—sales managers, accounting managers, and so on. People in this tier are generally referred to as line managers, because their responsibilities go in a direct line from the workers to the top managers. If sales are down, the sales manager takes the blame. If sales are up, the sales manager gets the praise. This is the line manager's main reason for existing, to ensure that the area he is managing is meeting expected performance goals. These are measurable quantities such as the number of new customers, the number of drains cleaned, or whatever the manager's sphere of responsibility encompasses.

Finally, there are first-level managers. These are the supervisors responsible for seeing that a small group of people complete their tasks. This manager has the most hands-on involvement and requires the most technical knowledge.

In the Roman army, there was a first-level manager, a leader for every eight men. This group of soldiers was called a contubernium. If the army lost a battle, the contubernium sergeants were executed, and a new sergeant for each one was assigned from the soldiers. Ten contubernia formed a centuria, which was commanded by a mid-level manager, a centurion. Though a centurion originally commanded about 83 men, this number later could reach 100. This became the generally accepted model for the approximate number of people a supervisor can handle, and likewise, the number of supervisors a middle manager can handle.

Of course, some disciplines need more managers, while many can get by with less. The latter guideline particularly works if there are large numbers of people doing very similar tasks.

Management styles have been discussed and dissected ad nauseam by many teachers and writers of business topics, but it all boils down to a scale: dictatorial on one end and democratic on the other. A dictatorial manager issues orders without consulting his or her workers, while a democratic manager allows the workers to decide what needs to be done, along with how and when the work should be done.

Neither of these extremes works well. On the dictatorial end of the scale, people being managed feel left out of any decision-making and end up resentful of the company—they feel used, as if they were machines. On the other end, if you allow the workers to decide everything, they'll usually only decide to do the more fun things and can end up ignoring important tasks that might be unpleasant or tedious.

Somewhere in the middle is a consultative management style, which takes into account the wishes, strengths, and weaknesses of employees while coaching and directing their efforts to achieve the company's goals and strategic plans. For each manager, the degree of autocracy and democracy is a bit different; for each employee, the sweet spot of how much he or she needs to be managed is a bit different. Some people work independently better than others, while some need to be managed more. The wise manager considers these differences in each worker to most effectively bolster productivity.

Each manager needs to develop his or her own style. It becomes a kind of character one might portray in a play. Of course it needs to contain elements of the person's true self, but it also needs to be a persona separate from one's self.

It is a bit like parenting: you show your chil-

Chapter 8

People 360

People are resources that, in the past, have been largely taken for granted by business leaders. They once thought that they only needed to hire people who were qualified to fill certain slots, and to perform tasks that needed to be done, and let it go at that. Human capital development and management is the phrase used now, and this shows how this approach has changed over the years. More than intellectual capital, human capital is critical for any organization.

People are no longer just slotted into place but are developed. Recognizing potential in people is what separates excellent person managers from mediocre ones. You can always train the right people to perform as you wish them to but you can never give enough training to someone who does not have the desire to succeed.

The first step in developing people is to do a skills gap analysis. You need to evaluate people, fairly and accurately, to figure out what they are good at and what they need help developing.

Before you can do this, you need to identify critical skills, those that the position requires excellence at, as separate from those that would be nice to have.

A skills gap analysis is effective when it is used on what personnel actually do, not on what they are trained to do. There are many formalized methods for doing this, and an entire industry is growing up around performing skills gap analyses. In essence, a skills gap analysis is a rating system that rates the employee based on his or her ability to do certain tasks. Naturally, some subjectivity slips in when evaluating employees, but efforts should be made to keep things as objective as possible.

Skills gap analyses reveal which employees or candidates truly have leadership potential, not merely those who would make adequate managers. By using a formal rating system, areas requiring improvement can be identified, and a certain prescription for training may be given instead of using a one-size-fits-all training regimen.

With the advent of ISO-9000, employee training and development has taken on a new mandate. Companies perform better and their products are of higher quality when all employees are formally trained and have a written and properly executed plan and procedure for carrying out tasks. It has been proven over and over that time spent on employee training and development is never wasted. Efficiencies, quality, and morale improve when properly defined and thought-out training plans are installed.

As a minimum, all employees need to be trained on the 4Ts of management: Tasks, Team, Target, and Timeline (see chapter 5) to understand the formalized way every project needs to be carried out. Even if it is sweeping the floor, a 4T approach is what every business needs to perform efficiently; and people in the organization need to understand how it applies to their job.

They also should be aware that they will be evaluated through a 4T management approach.

Businesses also need to recognize their employees' achievements. Employees' loyalty and drive to succeed comes from them understanding that they are a valuable part of the team. They need to know that that their contributions matter. One of the best ways to create those feelings of loyalty is to promote awards and recognition. Far more powerful than cash bonuses, recognition of employees engenders a team spirit in personnel. Be sure to have quantifiable standards and benchmarks from which to base your awards and achievement recognition. It is not a popularity contest; it's an appreciation of production. The lesson that you can't manage what you can't measure, as described in Chapter 7, applies to people just as it does to processes.

Finally, every business—no matter how small—should have a leadership development program. Even if you are a one-person business, having what we call VPA (vision, plan, action) for personal leadership development is important for any business to grow and improve. Have a firm vision of your leadership goals, plan how you intend to achieve those goals, put those plans in writing, and put them into action by starting at the beginning.

Google, the Internet search engine giant that brings in $23 billion per year, is annually voted one of the top employers in the United States. Google demands a lot from its employees, but it also gives them a lot. The employees get free food and drinks, free laundry service and in-house exercise equipment. The company also has an extremely strong recognition program. Employees can even award their coworkers cash bonuses if they think they deserve it—this is a popular perk.

The result is that Google gets its pick of the best candidates, its employees are far more productive than the industry norm, and its employees are fiercely loyal.

Google doesn't hire easily. It might take as many as 10 interviews to get hired. The company is in no rush to fill every slot, so it takes its time to make sure every slot is filled with a competent, loyal person who will understand (and fit into) the Google culture.

This is a good principle to follow. Never be in a rush to fill voids. Take your time to craft a great team. With it, you'll go far.

Businesses that have so-called people problems or turn into revolving doors for their employees fail at these very simple, straightforward principles. Businesses that use them have happy, productive, loyal employees. It's that simple. Large businesses all started small, often at a kitchen table or garage office. They got big by hiring the right people and cultivating teamwork, team spirit and loyalty. It works both ways: You expect a lot out of the employees, and you provide them a lot. Every manager has a role. If you expect greatness, you too must be willing to be great.

Chapter 9

Technology 360

Technology has so completely taken over the business world that it is important for the business manager or entrepreneur to be fully versed on its capabilities and uses.

Back in the 1970s, the staff of a typical small manufacturing company would include several secretaries; a person to handle accounts receivable, accounts payable, benefits and human resources; several engineers; several draftspeople; and at least two people assigned to production control. The front-office staff would number about a dozen (not including middle managers) in a typical company that averaged about $3–$5 million in annual revenue. By the year 2000, none of these jobs still existed.

The managers can accomplish all of those tasks independently, without the need of any staff. Technology has transformed the productivity of the white-collar worker; technological know-how has become a core skill of modern management.

In addition to accomplishing basic technical tasks, such as computer-aided design, production management, accounting, shipping, and so on, computer technology has opened up new and very exciting possibilities in business operations. Every manager or entrepreneur should understand these possibilities and be able to use them to his or her advantage. The future looks very bright indeed and a continual stream of new applications is introduced every year, increasing these capabilities even further.

Let's break down some of the aspects that the modern manager should be thoroughly familiar with into the "6 Cs" of technology:

Collaboration – There was a time when holding a meeting meant getting on an airplane, renting a car and meeting your client face-to-face in order to have your meeting. This is no longer true. Now we have online applications like GoToMeeting,1 where you can fill a virtual conference room with people from all over the world and collaborate live and in real-time. Each person can see the conference leader's computer screen, which presents and shares any desired presentations or graphical data (basically anything that can appear on a computer monitor).

If just simple screen-sharing is desired, there are free online tools like Join.me2 that can be switched on while talking on the telephone. Join.me allows a remote caller see exactly what's on your computer screen at any time.

Conference: If you wanted to speak to someone overseas 25 years ago, you had one choice: Ma Bell. To call from the US to Japan, for instance, cost about $1 per minute back in the 1980s. That made for very short and infrequent phone conferences.

Today, you can use computer conferencing using Skype3 or OoVoo,4 for free. Not only that, these services allow for video conferencing, so you can see the person you are talking to. Both of these services also allow you to call landlines or mobile telephones from your computer for pennies per minute.

Communications: Gone are letters with stamps that took days, sometimes weeks, to get somewhere. Also gone are FAX machines that sometimes did and sometimes did not yield read-able results. These days, with email and document sharing services like Google docs,5 you can share original quality documents instantly, anywhere in the world. Even the IRS allows you to file your taxes electronically online. The modern manager must be very well versed in the latest document sharing methods to stay in communication with his or her associates, suppliers and customers.

Contact management: Remember the Rolodex? How about business card files? Those are now quaint memories of the past. You may still see the term Rolodex used in job search descriptions such as "Need someone with a full Rolodex to in-troduce this product to the territory," implying they are looking for someone who has a complete net-work of business contacts within a certain area or industry. Actual Rolodexes are long gone though, having been replaced with simple-to-use databases for contacts. Act,6 and Batchbook7 are two simple ones, and Microsoft Outlook contains a fairly com-plete contact management component (along with other features like scheduling).

Client management: New software has taken over the business community to enable the management of clients. Easy invoicing and billing systems that do not require extensive accounting training are everywhere. Freshbooks8 is such an example, as along with the current most popular choice, Quickbooks.9 One simple and inexpensive piece of software can replace a team of bookkeepers and can be used by anyone.

Solve36010 is yet another significant type of client-management software. It tracks customer support and project management easily and intuitively, freeing employees charged with these tasks from having to engage in tedious recordkeeping, instead allowing employees to focus on the customer's needs. Customer support software is a major step ahead for businesses, and one the modern manager must be conversant in.

Commerce: It is even possible to automate commerce activities, such as buying, payment and shipment of products online, without direct input from clerks. Paypal11 and Google Checkout12 are two such online purchasing and banking systems. They allow customers to purchase and pay for products from online virtual stores, and services include calculating and collecting sales taxes, shipping fees, and providing the shipping department with a packing list and a shipping label with prepaid postage attached. All this is accomplished while the system is completely unattended.

These commerce systems can even ship the product without any input at all, provided the product is something that can be downloaded, such as an informational product or software. Your business can be open, selling and delivering products while you sleep.

Perhaps the most well thought out series of business applications is Google Apps.13 It has an entire series of effective, easy-to-use applications that are, in essence, free for the small business owner.

Automation for managers has freed them from so many time-consuming tasks, which in the past robbed managers of so much potential creative time. Modern managers need not have clerking staff, nor devote hours to recordkeeping. They can instead concentrate on those creative tasks that produce results. It looks as though these trends will continue as well. As a manager you will benefit by staying ahead of this curve instead of trying to park yourself at one point and not keeping up with ongoing advances.

Chapter 10

Networking 360

In today's world, networking skills are important to the manager and entrepreneur alike. Networking increases your own net worth and increases your value to the company you work for, whether your own company or someone else's. There was a time when companies wanted you to interface only with customers and suppliers, not competitors or people in other businesses in the same industry – but those days have gone the way of the electric typewriter, slide rule and drafting machine. The modern world demands that you stay up-to-date with industry trends and fellow industry personnel, and build new concepts of working together by harnessing the power of networking.

Like any other aspect of business, network-

ing requires the creation of a strategic plan to establish, manage and stay current with your contacts. Applying VPA (Vision, Plan, Action) to your
networking tasks is just as valid as applying it to
any other business project. If you plan to excel at
social networking, VPA can help you do so.

Begin by envisioning your network. Figure
out which people you'd love to have in it; envision
how it will improve your job performance. Once
you have your vision in your mind (don't forget to
also have it down on paper) then you can begin
your planning. Write out a networking plan and
follow this plan with action. Start actively carrying out your plan. Like any other VPA cycle, you
may have to make adjustments and changes as you
move along. That's OK. Just remember: plans are
nothing, planning is everything. Executing your
plan is how you turn your plans into reality.

There are a number of channels you should
pursue to broaden and strengthen your networks:

Online networking: Another beauty of the
internet is that it aids in connecting you with many
people, all over the world, who are in a position to
assist you on your business journey.

Social networking sites are an excellent way
to get started. Linked-In is the primary professional

networking site. Facebook is the second most significant. Through social networking, you can connect with industry experts, suppliers, potential customers, recognized technical experts, sales and marketing experts, financial people, and a whole bevy of other business professional experts.

Face2Face networking: In addition to your online friends and associates, your networking plan should also stress face-to-face networking contacts. By attending business conferences, trade shows, business networking events, chambers of commerce and similar networks, and other business-oriented events, you get a chance to "press the flesh" with fellow businesspeople. By associating with these fellow businesspeople, you can make friends, support each other's interests and careers, and generally associate with others who can relate to your situation. Meeting in-person brings with it a much more lasting and real experience than simply swapping emails, and because of this, it is important to network both online and off.

Networking has numerous advantages. Some of them include:

Finding new leads for your business: People like to carry out business with people they know — and knowing a lot of people, especially in your industry, means you know a lot of potential customers.

Raising your profile: Being known as someone who knows everyone is a significant boon to your own career and business profile with others. Whether they're right or wrong, people will naturally assume that you are well-versed in the industry if you know a lot of people in the industry and many people know you.

Free consultations: Knowing someone to ask when you have a problem is a huge advantage, especially if that someone is a respected member of the business community or the technical community of your industry. People are usually willing to offer free advice and suggestions to members of their personal networks.

Uncover new opportunities: Oftentimes you'll find out about new business opportunities or job opportunities in your networking circles. Keeping your eyes and ears open may lead you to things you never imagined when sitting alone in isolation.

Development of friendships: Networking introduces you to large communities of like-minded people, many of whom you will share experiences, concerns, problems, and solutions with. These are the kind of people you will find it easy to develop lasting personal friendships with.

Satisfaction from helping others: Never overlook the personal satisfaction and positive karmic influence that can be gained from helping others.

Effective networking is a skill you need to develop. The focus should be on developing quality contacts, rather than quantity. You should strive to add recognized experts, rising stars, and effective leaders to your business network. Obviously, this requires some research before pursuing contacts. With Internet search engines, this has become easy. Simply Google the people you know will be at events or online before contacting them and ask them about some aspect of their career or body of work. This shows that you really do have a genuine interest in adding yourself to their network. Sticking out your hand and asking, "Who are you and what do you do here?" won't win you any points if you're talking to the CEO of a major company.

Make your network a two-way street. Busy people dislike connecting with people who are only there to take from them. Networks are only effective if they are two-way streets. What can you offer this person that they can't get anywhere else?

Do you plan only to learn from them? How can knowing you benefit them? These are the kinds of questions you should think through before approaching a business leader.

One of the most effective ways to network is to join a networking group. One of the best of these is Entrepreneur21. Visit the website at www.Entrepreneur21.net.

Entrepreneur21 is an exclusive, online business networking platform for the professionals, leaders, and entrepreneurs of the twenty-first century. It was founded on the principle of entrepreneurs for entrepreneurs (E4E). Entrepreneur21 will be used by thousands of entrepreneurs worldwide to network, collaborate, conduct business, brainstorm, innovate, and help each other achieve success. Basic membership into Entrepreneur21 is complimentary and sponsored by the United States Global Enterprise Association (USGEA).

If you join this group, you'll have free access to many very successful entrepreneurs. You'll be able to pick their brains for great ideas, lean on them for advice regarding your own ideas, and forge ahead with the knowledge that their vast and successful business experience is on tap whenever you need it. Imagine the confidence and certainty you'll have knowing that those who have blazed the trail are right beside you, showing you the way.

Entrepreneur21 hosts an annual conference and get-together filled with speakers, professional businesspersons, successful entrepreneurs, and more. It is a life-changing experience to attend. You'll walk away motivated, energized, and filled with powerful and practical entrepreneurial information.

Chapter 11

Entrepreneurship 360

Being an entrepreneurial leader requires more than simply being a business manager. You need to develop and practice a larger skill set. An entrepreneur leader needs to be able to perform on many different levels, from long term strategic planning to execution of simple tasks, and do them all well. This leader must also have the desire and passion to do what it takes to make the business exceptional, and keep it there.

Success isn't simply arriving at the destination, it is an ongoing drive to keep the business successful.

Many entrepreneurs have shown the vision and drive required to get their chosen businesses to the top, only to have these endeavors come crashing down when they become distracted by other matters and take attention away from the business at hand.

Following are the 21 skills an entrepreneurial leader must have, why every leader must have them, and what you can do to achieve these skills.

1. Visionary: Entrepreneurs have a unique perspective that sets them apart. Having vision means being able to see what lies ahead. It means having the audacious dream of success. Entrepreneurs imagine what success looks like, smells like, tastes like, feels like and sounds like. Don't listen to your mother or teachers from the past chiding you for daydreaming – go ahead and daydream, but do it with purpose.

2. Ambitious: No entrepreneur is happy with a mundane outcome. Entrepreneurs are competitive, have a strong need for achievement, and believe in building something big out of nothing. This is a learned skill – you need to reject mediocrity and only allow yourself to accept the exceptional. Expect the exceptional and you will achieve it.

3. Creative: In modern-day life, the term "thinking outside the box" is overused. There really is no box – only historical records of what oth-

ers have done. Find your own path and follow it with the confident awareness that if you can envision something, you can achieve it. You will invent innovative solutions and bold marketing strategies.

4. Optimistic: Belief in the future is the very engine of entrepreneurial success. You constantly have negative thoughts and emotions thrown at you by your friends, relatives, and even that silly voice in your own head. These do you absolutely no good. Negative thoughts only hold you back; ignore them. Proceed and learn to make lemonade out of lemons.

Seek ways to transform every opportunity presented to you into a positive thing, rather than focusing only on the faults.

5. Leadership: Building winning teams is the focus of all successful entrepreneurs. Be a bold leader and people will follow. Having the confidence to lead others will take you far in business and in life. Don't worry: there is success enough to go around for all. Don't feel obligated to hog it all for yourself.

6. Intelligent: Not everyone is born with an exceptional IQ, but everyone can learn to intelligently solve problems, and anyone can acquire common sense. I'm sure you know more than one very

intelligent person who completely lacks common sense. The surprising thing is that these people often deny that they lack common sense, even though the evidence is all around them. It's relatively easy to develop formulaic methods for problem solving – think things through with a logical and creative approach.

7. Risk Taker: Entrepreneurs favor business opportunities that carry a moderate degree of calculated risk. They realize that the most return comes from the most risk, and so they're willing to put everything on the line for the right opportunity. Invest in a savings account and you'll end up with a safe investment, but very little return. Invest in a start-up company and your potential for enormous returns is high, but then again your chance for losing is also high. Entrepreneurs would rather invest and lose than sit around and watch their savings accounts stagnate.

8. Energetic: In spite of a bestselling information book back in the 70s and 80s, there is no "Lazy Man's Way to Riches." Entrepreneurship takes hard work and dedication. Entrepreneurs have the ability to work long hours and the desire to work until they finish their tasks.

Actions succeed, lack of actions always fail.

Getting up every morning with the idea that you will get a lot accomplished is the skill needed to make it as an entrepreneur.

9. Independent: To be an entrepreneur, you need to learn to be your own counsel. You don't need, nor should you seek approval from others. Those who get the most praise seek the least and vice-versa, those who seek the most receive the least. Entrepreneurs are individualists and self-starters who prefer to lead rather than follow. Again, this is a confidence issue. Have the confidence to continually move forward without the need for other's approval and you'll acquire more confidence as you achieve milestones along the way. It is a self-fulfilling prophecy.

10. Self-Motivated: Entrepreneurs never give up. They cheer themselves up when they are down and are decisive and confident of their ability to manage any situation. They are their own best friends and can look inside when they need to make a decision. They rely on their own abilities to solve any problem.

11. Passionate: Entrepreneurs love to work and truly believe in what they do. They derive pleasure from what they do. They'd probably be doing it even if they didn't get paid for doing it. That is

an important thing to consider when selecting a business. It matters that you care about what you are doing. Affinity for something can be cultivated. Consider someone playing the piano. It only gets fun when you start getting good. Practicing to get there can be a grind. Businesses are similar. Have the tenacity to continue through the tough parts until it becomes easier, and as it gets easier, it gets more fun.

12. Realistic: Making wise decisions means understanding reality and knowing when to adjust, adapt, improvise and modify your plans to accommodate a change of conditions.

These are the skills demonstrated when businesses are managed to be agile. Things change – they always have and they always will. How you adapt your business in light of those changes is what makes the difference between a successful entrepreneurship and a decaying one.

13. Sacrificing: Entrepreneurs are willing to make personal sacrifices to achieve their goals because they are fully committed to achieving their goals. This means sacrificing time and attention, as well as money. Famed guitarist Jeff "Skunk" Baxter, who played with Jimmy Hendrix, Steely Dan, and the Doobie Brothers, said that while all

of his friends were out on Friday nights having fun and chasing girls, he was home practicing guitar. However, after he got good enough, the girls began chasing him. Sacrificing today can reap enormous rewards tomorrow.

14. Persuasive: Having persuasion skills is an important requirement for an entrepreneur. Obtaining funding, selling your product, team building, and just about every other aspect of a business hinges on having the power of persuasion. This takes a dose of charisma. Like the other skills listed here, persuasion can be learned, nurtured, practiced, and improved. These skills aren't a fixed quality that people must be born with.

15. Tenacious: Entrepreneurs believe in sticking to their goal, even it means doing things differently. Calvin Coolidge said it best when he said: "Nothing in this world can take the place of persistence. Talent will not; nothing is more common than unsuccessful people with talent. Genius will not; unrewarded genius is almost a proverb. Education will not; the world is full of educated derelicts. Persistence and determination alone are omnipotent. The slogan 'press on' has solved and always will solve the problems of the human race."

16. Courageous: By looking failure in the

face, and saying, "NO – not on my watch," entre-preneurs separate themselves from the majority of the people occupying office cubicles in big build-ings around the world. Most people think: "What if I fail, what about if this or if that or....?" Did you realize that over 98% of the things people worry about will never come to pass? All of that worry is futile, and the fastest way to bring about some-thing negative is to dwell on it. The successful en-trepreneur faces new challenges with a smile.

17. Adaptable: One of the skills entrepre-neurs possess is adaptability; they are always pre-pared and able to adapt to new conditions and situ-ations. As with other skills listed here, adaptabil-ity is a learned quality. It comes from a combina-tion of other skills, such as tenacity, intelligence, and realism. Mix in a healthy dose of self-confi-dence to create adaptability.

18. Ethical: Entrepreneurs are never suc-cessful by being unethical. Possessing ethics is a critical skill. The press and moviemakers love to make it seem as if businesspeople are all thieves and liars, but in real life, only those with ethics survive. It's easy to be ethical in the good times, but if you can remain ethical in spite of unfavor-able conditions, you will always win out as an en-

trepreneur.

19. Self-controlled and Disciplined: Staying focused on your vision and achieving success as an entrepreneur requires self-control. It's undoubtedly easier to leave work early when you are working for yourself, but you can't do this if you expect to succeed. You need to constantly remind yourself of your goals, know that you're on the path to achieving them, and exert self-discipline in order to accomplish greatness. The more you practice discipline and control the better you get.

20. Honest and Trustworthy: When your employees, suppliers and customer know they can rely on you, this is another hallmark of a successful entrepreneur.

Certainly people will do business with you if you're not, but they'll look for every excuse under the sun to find someone else if they don't trust you. You can contrast that with the loyalty you'll get from the people who do trust you.

21. The entrepreneur needs to be a strategic thinker. He or she needs to be able to take a look from 10,000 feet, see the big picture, and understand how the business fits into its surrounding conditions and marketplace. This need not be

done every day, but the successful entrepreneur is able to step back from the day-to-day activities of keeping the business afloat and look at the big picture.

While it is not necessary to become world class at every entrepreneurial skill to be a successful entrepreneurial leader, you should be familiar with each and work on developing each to the best of your ability. You can rely on associates, networks of other professionals, partners, and trusted confidants to bolster your skills in the areas where you may be lacking. Having an awareness of what is expected of you and what you need to improve is what makes the difference between being an entrepreneurial leader or a lifetime business manager.

We have gone past the age when managers had to be technicians. Modern technology takes care of many of the mundane tasks that managers once had to either do themselves or to delegate to staff. Today companies pay their top-level for what they know and for knowing how to get it done. It is far more important to know what needs to be done than it is to know how to do it.

The sophistication of management in the 21st century has increased enormously from what it was only a generation ago. At one time, being a jack-of-all-trades branded you as mediocre, but today it elevates you. If you get paid for what you know, there is no limit to your earning potential. If you get paid for what you do, it becomes just trading hours for money. Recognize which opportunity is right for you.

So be a thinker, not just a doer. Think not just about yourself and your tasks; think for others around you, your family, your coworkers, your subordinates, and especially for your organization as a whole. This will make a huge impact on your thought process and affect your actions for the better. When you think universally, your actions and your impact will have a magnitude more powerful than if you think only about your own needs.

Thinking is the hardest work there is, which is probably the reason why so few engage in it.

– Henry Ford

About the Author

Dr. Shaan Senthil Kumar is chairman of iGLOBAL Investment Group, an international angel investment and technology incubation house. Dr. Kumar is also the founder and CEO of California InterContinental University, a globally recognized and nationally accredited university offering bachelor, master, and doctoral degree programs. In 2007, Dr. Kumar was appointed chairman of the United States Global Entrepreneurs (USGEA) Association, a nonprofit organization that promotes and nurtures entrepreneurs worldwide. The association was formed in Silicon Valley in 1999.

In 2003, Dr. Kumar was president and CEO of NETed Inc., an e-learning technology and services company, which is a division of Benchmark Online Pte. Ltd., funded by the Singapore Economic Development Board.

At the beginning of his career as a serial technology-focused entrepreneur, Dr. Kumar gained intensive experience in designing and patenting many processes and technologies. He was also involved in developing enterprise software, IT services, ERP solutions, and Internet business ventures. He has traveled to hundreds of cities worldwide in more than twenty-five countries, and is currently a resident of three countries.

He also serves on the board of H2B Studios, a "Hollywood 2 Bollywood" cross-cultural film production and entertainment company.

In 2004, he served as the chairman of eVisions, Q-Soft, and EdNET Solutions & Technology Group. He also served as a committee member for numerous boards including the International Bioinformatics Research Academy (iBRA) in Silicon Valley, ERM Anywhere.com, and the SunMicrosystems Asia Pacific Technology Review Committee. Prior to these activities, Dr. Kumar was a distinguished speaker, an IT evangelist, and a global partner of Microsoft Worldwide.

As a global entrepreneur and strategic angel investor, Dr. Kumar has secured investments for many high-tech and software companies. Some companies were acquired by large firms, becoming successful and going public under his leadership. His expertise and innovative thinking set the stage for the rapid development of existing companies, enabling them to reach new heights. He also enabled emerging enterprises to flourish in the global arena.

Dr. Kumar has tremendous experience in mergers and acquisitions, global franchise development, and establishing strategic partnerships and joint ventures across multiple industries.

He has offered solutions and services to many industries, such as banking, telecommunications, pharmaceuticals, health care, higher education, manufacturing, and government. His passion and expertise are in the fields of IT, entrepreneurial Internet startups, higher education, media, and entertainment businesses.

Dr. Kumar has authored many technical books, journals, and articles since 1996. He is currently developing several books in the *Just-N-Hour* series. An educator and social entrepreneur, Dr. Kumar started the K-Foundation, or Knowledge Foundation, which contributes to social causes such as the empowerment of women and child education programs. He has provided scholarships and grants to students worldwide and aspires to provide affordable educational and career development opportunities to thousands globally.

Dr. Kumar has a doctorate in business administration with an emphasis in entrepreneurship and management, an MBA in marketing and quantitative methods, and a Bachelor of Engineering in electronics and communications. He lives with his family in Diamond Bar, California.

A Handbook for
GLOBAL
Entrepreneurs

Vision Brilliance Success™

Dr. Shaan Kumar

Vision Brilliance Success by Dr. Shaan Kumar is the new breakout manual for people in all occupations who have an urge to become entrepreneurs and achieve success. It is for people who have already started their business on a small scale and wish to expand globally as well as professional leaders who want to become entrepreneurs. This book provides specific instructions for how to achieve your entrepreneurial goals.

Vision Brilliance Success by Dr. Shaan Kumar. ISBN 978-1460904268, 322 pages. Published by K-Publications, 2011

Acknowledgments

First, I'd like to thank my family for giving me the strength to work long hours to achieve my vision. I spent many hours after work, on weekends, and on holidays to complete this book, and I could not have done it without their blessings and support.

I'd also like to give special thanks to Jeff Spira. Jeff and I worked closely together on this project to ensure that readers of this book learn the value of having a dream and laying the foundation to achieve their goals.

Last, but not least, I'd like to thank Andrea Clarke, Robert Leonard, Kevin Vyas, and Brian Sanchez who contributed to this project. They each offered a unique perspective on the finished product.